PLAINSIGHT

JUSTIN RUNGE

PLAINSIGHT

JUSTIN RUNGE

NEW MICHIGAN PRESS
TUCSON, ARIZONA

NEW MICHIGAN PRESS
DEPT OF ENGLISH, P. O. BOX 210067
UNIVERSITY OF ARIZONA
TUCSON, AZ 85721-0067

<http://newmichiganpress.com/nmp>

Orders and queries to nmp@thediagram.com.

Copyright © 2012 by Justin Runge.
All rights reserved.

ISBN 978-1-934832-38-7. FIRST PRINTING.

Printed in the United States of America.

Design by Ander Monson.

Cover image by Robert Josiah Bingaman, *Untitled*, 2010.

CONTENTS

Plainsight   1

Acknowledgments   41

It is poetic, musical…of fugues without a skeleton.
Melancholy with vertabrae. That is why I can't live here.

Federico Garcia Lorca

454

Locked land
is still water-
drawn. Bridges
are the army
corps' craft
work here,
of similar
disposition
to the men
riveting them.
Build to a sea
level given
from survey
after survey.
To demarcate
goes horizon
far. The lines
at times appear
after mowing.
And from mid-
bridge. Merge
west. The sun
confronts all
arrivals. Flanks
of coal-burning

engines gargoyle
at the entrance.
Monumenting
the effort to blur
through this.
How fast cattle.
Standing laws
keep casinos
to the other
side, so Iowa
gets to glitter.
Tractor trailers
void stomachs
upon stockyards.
Mile one is true
and humorless.
And as silent
as can be, divide
by neighbor-
hoods bullied
into the interstate.

432

Young ones
howl from

a ball pit.
The outlet
embraces
like a cave.
As Roman
decay was
built in. A day
of snooping
through wind-
ows, or owl
necks always,
like jar tops,
twisting past.
This, haunted
by merchants
who hawk
deformed
corduroy over-
alls, archaic
floppy disk
edutainment.
Fed by its own
water tower.
Kept warm
by a shawl
of parking lot
pulled up to
hide acne scars.

The cars signal
their leaving
with seizure
episodes, rattle.
Two functions
here: departure
and effluvia.
The food court,
a failed utopia.
A place to rid
oneself. Weight
loss retail space
available. Women
in the karate suite
practice breaking
noses. Later walk
to nylon fire sale.

426

Grama field
is in italics,
emphasizes
the horizon-
tal current

of air. No
pause. Burg
is Atlantean
in a mirage
from heat
lying water
on pavement.
Slow to rise.
Structures
push against
the ground,
stand, tired
sawhorses.
Ranch homes
cower, afraid
to shoulder
another story.
A diamond
is ignored
in its weeds.
No. Boys
shadow play
an inning,
dust bases
off in blasé
archeology.
Are safe left

alone. Rarity
of pavement.
Roads forget
to be named,
so as not to
fray, lattice
a grid, tight
as two hands
churching.

423

Each barrel
greeds up
high beam,
moon, then
shines white
like miracle.
Antennae
begin here's
irrefutable
tempo. Their
red pulsation
in triplicate,
as vertical as
shirt buttons.

Kept in even
pace, pylons,
tines along
the dashes
delineating
lanes. Bathed
in effulgent
wash of work
light, a road
crew, mouths
masked, super-
vise steamroll
progress. As if
to greet some-
thing unearthing.
On the only hill-
top, a temple,
glass and rafter.
Like ascension
paused, resting.
Mile markers
bead by, rosary.
Turn signal
clicks point
and counter-
point talk
radio patter.

420

Signs ex-
clamatory
with exits.
Here. Here.
Windbreak
a bulwark
for the cattle
scatter. Plot
of car parts
is growing
rust, is not
the antique
store it wants
to be. Porn
Barn, World
War II Library
and Museum
once a truck
stop. Still,
three more
gas stations
for all those
who cannot
or won't stay.
Without hills,

the town still
hides, behind
grain elevators,
quiet as cud-
chewing, fume
passing through
a screen door
kept latched,
never slapped.
The basketball
hoops driven
into concrete
are gratuitous.

409

Of dozens
filling front
seat legroom,
a body shop
receipt gets
plucked out
by carjacking
crosswind,
rips across

the redacted
October crop,
a shot goose
skipping, just
blown. Apart-
ments, board
game barren.
No one buys
trees for them.
Clothing on
lines break
small sound
barriers, pop
at a terse gust.
Little brothers
smoking, sun-
lit vampires
lain in empty
acres. Bigger
brothers recon
on bikes. On
tracks, Penny
Savers flit. Ant
hill and its BBs.
A neighbor's
grill is a blanket
scent. The kids

upwind of it,
obfuscating.

397

Jagged graph-
like skyline
shows a city
that peaked
once. One
skyscraper,
limestone,
rust-domed,
blue bronze
sower over-
seeing plains.
Easy to make
this pinnacle
a turning point
or a bull's-eye.
A law passed
presses the rest
groundward,
says no taller
than. Expansion

must move then
like lungs, out-
ward, towards
turbines barely
able to recall
predecessors,
towards Cold
War air force
base housing
reincorporated.
Arterials dead
end in the out-
skirts. Annex-
ation is a hem.
Highways plow
through pasture.
Silos increase
their ambition.

353

Now, a water
tower bullies
the scape. This
one, in hot air

balloon getup.
Quickly, fast
food options,
stanchion sky.
Windbreaks
along parcels
say *we got you
surrounded* in
a posse drawl.
Lots of ammo
in the big box
store. Parking
lot perforates
a barn shape.
Still, corrals.
Carts, sparse
livestock loose
on the periphery.
Off-ramp motel
chains. Days,
Motor, Com-
fort Inn. Truck
grunts can't
pass the ply
of curtains.
Smell of all
the invisible

gas expelled
without an air-
ship to buoy.
Sour cubic tons.
Scratch ticket
mutilated, so
soon useless,
papier collé
against gravel.
Stop for snacks.
Unisex bathroom,
humid as June.

352

Kid platoons
in a cornfield,
detasseling.
Their hands,
like locusts,
fidget plague,
but set stalks
to blossom.
Idle pivots

are plesiosaur
skeletons sat
in the field,
fluke echoes
of here's act-
ual natural
history. Once
a sea. Rain
runoff coughs
flecked eras.
Weapon tips,
behemoth bone
shards worked
back like seeds
into soil, under
sneaker soles.
Noon held
aloft. The hay
stacked with
sack lunch
ate bleeding
from razor-
like leaves.
Four dogs
running rings
into the dirt

driveway
where a bus
idles evenings
for the flood
of preteens.
Dust plumes
with departure,
a dissolve.

291

Birch trees
unemployed
on the creek
shore. Limit
load one ton
on its bridge.
This stretch
was elected
for bisection,
so its small
glitches go
below unfelt.
Curt names,
Germanic.

Rock. Elk.
The rivulets,
in dialect,
homonymic
for neck pain,
clefts bent,
sedentary
and asleep.
Driven star
posts node
high-tensile
barbed-wire
into maplines.
Draped, they
are heavy with.
Are frozen into.
Winter flanks,
dun, crystal-
line. August
acre's mono-
culture green
is now vast
as dishwater,
camera film
sprung early,
washed out.

272

Trains incise
town no more
than five, six
minutes apart,
They're bound
for empty, then
for mountains
that fold, rise,
like bread loaf.
Stone, grain,
ethanol tank,
some graffiti
go with them.

270

Monument,
straddling
four lanes,
is a majestic
overpass.
Duo of steel
pegasi book-

end on top.
Families
arrive there
by accident.
A re-enactor
tears tickets
at the mouth
of an escalator
lancet-arched
in video. Ear-
phones pipe
in ambiance
of calf bawl,
axel clatter,
the gravely
old narrator.
The campfire
is fiberglass
and begs one
to mime heat.
The volume
is kept low
for the goers
to focus on
wandering.
Once, it was
bootfeet that

wore down
the continent.
But a placard
asserts speed
is the victory.
Underneath,
a peephole
to the Dwight
D. Eisenhower
Nat'l System
of Interstate
and Defense.

259

A queue
curls into
the giant
hog lot.
Air here
involves
all senses.
The retch
of farrow
laid over

constant
pig burble.
The scent,
at once new
and an end,
fogs off
the clods
of ordure
and suffuses
the unfurled
cloudiness
of so many
steaming
things. Huff
of nostrils
atomizing,
feces heat,
blood heat,
the killing
floor hosed.
If the roof
tore off
and rose,
the piggery
would vapor
like coffee
from a mug,

like geese
spooked up,
like ghosts
set free.

237

Stadium
lights dawn
over a feed-
lot, football
fields long.
Sucklings
plug maws
to mothers.
Their job
is to feed
efficiently.
Quartered
chambers
all process.
A village
surrounds
the factory,
forms a sort

of perimeter.
Expectant
of sprawl,
their dead
end streets
are battened.
The lowing
of its homes
each morning.
The sleeping
things here,
all standing.

230

Pheasant
lift like hats
from wheat
in its half-life.
Thunder, then.
Lead-riddled
bird tumble,
a reminder
of gravity.
From copse,

one anomaly,
Orion, vest
loud orange,
plods en route
to the corpse,
guts it, hands
puppeteering.
Decay's change.
Crops, erased.

222

Mildly, a boo.
Gently-spread
air rifle pellets
over a torso.
Calliope mu-
zak polluting
in big mono.
Town square
time travels
in the flood
lights. Less
sulk and sag.
Men off work,

walkeating.
They crook
dog-curious
for a corncob,
which tilts
the air force
brass band.
Amphitheatre
is fat, mothy.
Same audience
a housefire has.
The children
freely wander
to the trash
barrels, syrupy.
Mothers yawn
with turnstile
arms. Surprise.
Sun sets behind
everyone's back.

196

In stretches,
the highway

runs next
to a rapid
dragging
framework
of side cars
coal-heavy.
Scarves
of carbon
trail, fade.
The speed
changes
speed, hum-
mingbirds.
At the stop,
a striped arm
claps down,
wags stiff
to the chug
and draft
(so slight
the shake,
parallel to
commotion
and its blur,
juxtaposed).
A fluttering
zoetrope,

horse legs
just a strobe
below body.
Flicker, bell,
and whistle.

164

In soy fields,
stray stalks
of corn poke
up, periscopic.
How weeds
ruin a plane.
This plain,
with wave-
lets breaking,
ripples firm
to the foot,
make sense
of calenture.
A thresher's
baleen fills
with krill-
like grain,

and behind,
balers nest
what's dead,
what's left.
At dusk, will-
o'-the-wisp
trucks flick
for home.

143

The Midwest
grows black
hole-massive.
Just enough
tilting vista
there to hide
its few things,
swung behind
and clutched.
Every curve
takes minutes,
which disputes
this as ocean.

Basic waves,
two or three
fingers. Who
these people
are. Counties
gather them
like spilled
collectibles.
Horse adrift
does not see
a thorn-thick
fence until
it is fenced.
Everything
is crushed
by this sky,
as if a vise
grip forms
from ground
and it. Dark
mouth. Posts
but no lights.
Some hungry
grazer chews
all the bulbs
from the stems.

126

What's frozen
thaws, so that
preservations
wither. House
wood weathers,
gets no new
paint. Families
are dwindling.
The last gas
station expects
only elderly,
brews coffee.
Measurement
here takes time
as shape. Years,
their segments.
At sixty-five
MPH, a town
is ten seconds.
The post office,
a swift swan song.
Ruins of houses,
barns, trailers.
Towns of twenty.

Highway seized
as main street.
Propane tanks
slender as war-
heads sit next
to corrugated
steel everything.

107

Exed, extra
2x4s cross-
bar a drunk
silo, brace.
It's a jigsaw
toy mussed,
pieces gone,
pieces lost,
so the osiers
of its skirt
boning show.
(If any find
height here,
they shake

and slouch,
a discomfort
of corsetry;
some, like
linebackers,
crouch, legs
and arm
in a tripod
to embrace
any onrush.)
Tree limbs
jut like bone
from a tear.
When an elm
is diseased
from inside,
it will forget
give, so break
like a fullback
with no tackle.
Stakes teach
saplings how
to take wind,
not to bend.
backbone.

88

Rigs sleep
like steeds
hitched up.
Pneumatic
snort. Semis
are waking
with sound
like neighs.
A feeding
teen, spray
of sunflower
seed shells
from inside
a cargo van.
Driver deep
knee bends
and ambulates
mid-marathon
while a game
of tag swarms
around steel
community
college art—
here made
oxidizing

wreckage
(an incident
of aesthetic
to interrupt
the flushing
toilet white
noise). Ears
pressed
to crooks,
how one uses
sea shells,
for a shh.
Passengers,
their cubist
necks bent.
A hundred
miles, then
next rest.

55

Zipper tooth
shelter belts
secrete geese,
which spray

into the clear
designation
of above
at an air
horn yowl.
Only winter
sees surface
reflect sky,
both dirty
white. Out
in the open,
the fowl
spindrift.
A squirm
of muscae
volitantes
flocks with
this flock,
amoebic, in
marionettic
movement,
irreal glide.
Against taut
cyclorama
the wires
must hide.
Plain sight.

Afforest-
ation foot-
lights this
theater full
of floating.

20

Hills are slow,
bluffs sudden.
SUVs instead
of pack mules
corkscrew up.
At the top,
a plaque notes
how one man
died. A lone
helicopter low
at the plateau
tip. Sagebrush
beating ictus
to its bluster.
An older man
hardly shaken,
bent on a bench.

Scrub crush
under squeal
of approaching
babies björned.
Camper horn
peals off a far
aiguille. Math
is somewhere
in the still
before echo.
Strata, itself
reverberations,
like a ruler.
A multi-tiered
rod demarcates
how curious
mobs eroded
rock more
effectively
than the past
water could.

ACKNOWLEDGMENTS

Many thanks to the editors of the publications where these poems first appeared, some in altered versions:

"20," "55," "409," and "432" in *SOFTBLOW*, Spring 2010
"196," "222," and "230" in *Midwestern Gothic*, Issue 6
"259" in *Lines + Stars*, Vol. 4 No. 3
"353," "352," and "88" in *Umbrella Factory*, March 2010
"426" in *Prick of the Spindle*, Vol. 4.1
"454" in *elimae*, May 2010

JUSTIN RUNGE was born in Omaha, Nebraska, and currently lives in Lawrence, Kansas, where he serves as Poetry Editor of *Parcel*. Poems of his have appeared in *DIAGRAM*, *Linebreak*, *The Journal*, and elsewhere. He can be found at <www.justinrunge.me>.

༄ ༄

COLOPHON

Text is set in a digital version of Jenson, designed by Robert Slimbach in 1996, and based on the work of punchcutter, printer, and publisher Nicolas Jenson. The titles are in Futura.

NEW MICHIGAN PRESS, based in Tucson, Arizona, prints poetry and prose chapbooks, especially work that transcends traditional genre. Together with DIAGRAM, NMP sponsors a yearly chapbook competition.

DIAGRAM, a journal of text, art, and schematic, is published bimonthly at THEDIAGRAM.COM. Periodic print anthologies are available from the New Michigan Press at NEWMICHIGANPRESS.COM/NMP.

www.ingramcontent.com/pod-product-compliance
Lightning Source LLC
Chambersburg PA
CBHW031504040426
42444CB00007B/1200